The Promised
Key

The Promised
Key

Introduction
W. Gabriel Selassie I, Ph.D.

Leonard Percival Howell

For Simon Wiltz, AIA, NCARB
(1946 – 2010)
Professor, Emeritus Prairie View A & M University of Texas
School of Architecture
"Simon, you pointed me toward the light in Egypt."

Table of Contents

Introduction

*T*he *Promised Key,* written in 1930 by Leonard P. Howell aka G.G. Maragh is a little known treatise on the religion of African Diasporic blacks that emerged in Jamaica during a period of mass unrest in the 1930's. The time period was ripe for civil disobedience as the global economic depression had began to erode public confidence in governments worldwide. Great Britain ruled Jamaica first in absentia and later as a subjugated colony. British Colonial officials and their Jamaican intermediaries cared little for its people and most black Jamaicans eked out a meager life on subsistence farming or working as poverty wage earners.[1] To make matters worse massive dislocations from a series of hurricanes made the life on the Island unlivable throughout many months of the year.

Caribbean and North America slaves developed a sense of black consciousness often rooted most notably in *Ethiopianism.* The mythology of Ethiopianism was designed to unify blacks around a shared vision of repatriation to Africa or in some cases to live in peace and freedom and in the dignity of being

African on the very land they were enslaved.[2] In many ways Rastafari is a continuance of the struggle of people of African descent to make sense out of a world that offers circumscribed opportunity and no security. It along with Marcus Garvey's Black Nationalist movement offered blacks a sense of purpose, dignity and belief in a world that is Afrocentric at its core.

Howell's ministry emerged in Jamaica in the early 1930's at a time when conditions for its black population were at an all time low. In particular rural blacks were trapped in a cycle of poverty and exploitation that had not subsided since slavery. One of the seminal moments for Howell was the Tampico Hurricane of 1933. The Hurricane that passed through Jamaica was a series of storms initially observed on July 14 near St. Kitts. The storm dropped 9 inches or 230mm of rain and led to washouts and massive flooding, mudslides and disruptions in Kingston. The tropical storm wreaked havoc for rural villagers and demonstrated to the poor masses that relief from their misery would not come by the hands of the colonial administration. Howell would be particularly effective in preaching to the working class victims of the storm season. He was particularly successful with the villagers of St. Thomas Parish where the storms were most devastating.

Jamaica & European Slavery

St. Thomas is located in the southeast region of Jamaica. The parish is roughly 742.8 square kilometers and is considered Jamaica's ninth largest parish. The region is mountainous and particularly susceptible to mudslides. Its mountain ranges include the Port Royal, the Queensbury Ridge and Yallahs Hill. The Blue Mountains located in the North played a pivotal role, as they became home to maroon slaves that escaped their Spanish, English and French captors. Maroons gained their freedom through years of struggle by engaging the British military in a grueling and protracted guerilla war. Although the Maroons were African they were Jamaica's first true nationalists; they played a pivotal role in the formation of Jamaican national identity that became evident in the protestations against English colonial rule of the island.

In order to understand the role that Jamaican nationalist identity played in the formation of Howell's and other early Rastafarian thinking we must understand the role that European slavery played on the island and how it shaped early revolutionary thinking by the Africans brought to the island.

Jamaica and other West Indian islands are unique in world history in that they were established solely for the purpose of making and exporting sugar. Sugar was the leading economic engine that led to the accumulation of vast wealth for Europeans in the 18th and 19th centuries. Originally from the Middle East, sugar was produced in small quantities on the coast of the eastern Atlantic and typically only enjoyed by the wealthiest Europeans. But once sugar production was established in the West Indies it became a commodity of necessity in the diets of ordinary Europeans and thus the demand for sugar became insatiable.[3] The French colony of Saint-Domingue (Haiti) became the leading global sugar producer along with its competitor English Jamaica in the 18th century. Jamaica, by 1830 contained 320,000 black slaves or more than half the total of the British sugar colonies. In effect, Jamaica was the largest sugar colony in the British Empire.[4]

Christopher Columbus sailing under the Spanish flag landed on the Island of Jamaica in 1494. There he met both Arawak and Taino Indians people, who had settled on the island of Jamaica between 4000 and 1000 BC. During the year of Columbus' arrival, there were more than 200 Indigenous villages. Columbus unleashed a torrent of murder and villainy unparalleled in human history. For example, on the Island of Haiti Columbus used attack dogs-mastiff and greyhounds to terrorize the Native population. It is presumed by forensic evidence that dogs were allowed not just to terrorize but allowed to feast on the captured Indians.[5] By the time the Spanish had completed their "civilizing" mission they had wiped out the Indian population on the Jamaican island and only seventy-four Indians were estimated to be alive in 1611.[6] When the English captured Jamaica in 1655, the Spanish colonists fled after freeing their slaves. The slaves dispersed into the mountains, joining the maroons, those who had previously escaped from the Spanish to live with the remaining Tainos. These maroon communities were staunch defenders of their freedom.

The creation of the English plantation system for the singular purposes of capitalist exploitation marked the island as a haven for despots and barbarism. Orlando Patterson, a historian of Jamaican and world slavery noted that Jamaican society once established quickly became nothing less than "a monstrous distortion of human society."[7] Living on the Islands was characterized as intolerable for most white Europeans. Tropical fever, pestilence, poor weather, lack of an educated citizenry, few females for marriage, incompetent and deceitful officials, breakdown in morality and religion all worked to make life on the Island for white Europeans unlivable. Yet, this is the setting that the European introduced the African. At the root of this distorted society lay in "absenteeism." Absenteeism was an informal system where wealthy planters and merchants spent the bulk of their time in their countries of origin to take advantage of the luxuries of home living. One of absenteeism's greatest injuries was the lack of schools. The planter class viewed education with utter contempt and when necessary sent their children to England to be educated. Most of these young men and women did not return.[8] The absence of educated people on the island directly resulted in the breakdown of religion and morality among the resident whites since the local leaders were the most profligate people imaginable.[9] This set an unfortunate precedent that during colonial rule education of the masses was substandard and only prepared children for employment as state workers.

Unlike the highly economically and socially integrated slave system in the United States Jamaican slave society was loosely integrated. Absenteeism was a poorly managed and organized system of exploitation whereby social controls were minimal except through coercion. Patterson noted, "Jamaica was a *plantocratic* society par excellence."[10] In this light Jamaican society should be viewed as a collection of autonomous plantations, each a self-contained community with its internal mechanisms of power, than as a total social system characteristic of the United States plantation system. Typically the management of the estate was left to the whims of the overseers, many who forced the slaves to work far more hours than necessary to maintain human wellbeing. The irony is that overworking slaves, while depleting the capital investment in human chattel, procured high annual returns. This was done because the overseers were typically paid on a commission basis and crop yields were essential for profits. Overworked slaves died quickly and had to be replaced by more slaves, initiating a vicious cycle whereby slaves were constantly being introduced to the island.

Slaves in Jamaica generally lived in horrid conditions. Slave huts were arranged to resemble those of an African village. These one room daub and wattle huts were meager and disease ridden. Slave possessions amounted to a few wooden bowls, calabashes, wooden mortar and pestle, sometimes a crude bed but most slaves slept on the ground. Food was scarce and medical care provided by the planters non-existent, except that which could be administered by an African healer. Housing was always an acute problem with the increase in the number of slaves introduced on the island.

The total for the slave population are as follows:

Slave Population

1658: 1,400

1703: 45,000

1730: 74,525

1745: 112,428

1795: 291,000

1834: 311,070

Secular education for slaves as well as whites was non-existent nor were slaves in Jamaica given any form of religious education. The Church itself was incompetent and cynical and extremely intolerant of other denominations.[11] Most planters believed that slaves were incapable of understanding the complexities of Christian worship and therefore refrained from offering even a modicum of Christian religious services. However, by the late 19th century African American Baptists were most successful in converting slaves to Christianity. This was in part because of an American preacher named George Liele, and ex-American slave that come to Jamaica in 1784. Moses Baker, also an American black, who was baptized by Liele had success in St. James Parish.[12]

Because Christianity was not a plantation institution as it had been in America African religious practices were able to take hold on the island. In particular Obeah and Myalism. Obeah is a term used to refer to African folk magic and religious practices developed among West African slaves, specifically of Igbo origin. Obeah is similar to other Afro-American religions including Palo, Vodou, Santería, and Hoodoo. Myalism, on the other hand, is a communal practice, which involves a group of persons performing a unique dance ritual with the central figure, being the Myal-Man or "Doctor." Obeah men and Myalism practitioners were an active part of religious life in Jamaica for centuries.

Rebellion was a constant feature of Jamaican slave society. The most famous of these was the first Maroon War that lasted 15 years beginning about 1725. Akan tribesman almost uniformly instigated slave rebellions during the 17th century. These tribal warriors came from highly militaristic regimes and were skilled in jungle warfare. Obeah featured prominently in Jamaican slave rebellions especially among the Akan from the Gold Coast who led the slave uprising of 1760. I should note here that Akan slaves would make up the bulk of Maroon soldiers of Jamaica. Europeans viewed the Akan as so rebellious that a bill was introduced to restrain their importation to the Island in 1765. This failed. Researchers of Maroon descendants have noted the significant degree of Akan cultural survival traits among them.

These escaped Maroon slaves were akin to escaped slaves in North America who allied with Native America in Florida, who established free Seminole villages through much of Spanish Florida. The name is most likely derived from the Spanish word *cimarrón* literally meaning "feral animal, fugitive, runaway." A 1788 Jamaican census established at least 1,400 Maroons among a population of 250,100 slaves and 10,000 free blacks, and 30,000 whites.[13]

The British Crown spent considerable money and effort to eradicate the Maroon presence. The English were unsuccessful in subduing the Maroon communities due, in large part, to the nature of guerrilla warfare and the tenacity of leadership. Fighting between the English and Maroons ended with Peace or "Blood" Treaty of 1738. While the English and Maroon conflicts were to end these communities had established beyond a doubt that black communities with an African oriented culture were not only viable but could stand off a European power.

The harsh cruelties of slavery had a dramatic effect on creating the conditions that allowed for a growing nascent Jamaican nationalist movement. Leonard Howell, Marcus Garvey and other West Indians were part of the rebellious tradition that sought dignity over profits and African freedom over slavery.

Leonard Howell

What we know about the life of Leonard P. Howell is minimal. Most of the information about him is largely based his personal accounts allegedly told to newspaper reporters. We also have a few surviving family stories that have worked their way into becoming family lore. What we do know is the following. Leonard Percival Howell was born in May Crawie, Jamaica on June 16, 1898. Howell's father, Charles Theophilus Howell was both a peasant landowner and tailor and his mother, Clementina Bennett, was an agricultural laborer.[14] His early life was lived no different than any other young black child growing up in Jamaica in the late 19th century and hardly suggests that Howell would go on to lay the theological foundation for a movement that today spans the globe.

Sometime around 1918 Howell arrived in Colon, Panama. It is unclear as to what Howell's ambitions were in Panama but it's likely he was drawn there by the availability of work. Many immigrants from other countries had come to Panama during the 1910's to find work building the Panama Canal that opened on August 15, 1914. He might have also been part of the Jamaican war contingent- the British West Indies Regiment formalized by Army Order number 4 of 1916-that had been mustered into service for World War I.

After several trips back and forth to Jamaica, Howell stated that he joined the U.S. Army Transport Service and was sent to New York in October 1918. Prior the First World War the U.S. Army had been heavily scrutinized for the way it transported goods and services since the invasion of Cuba in the Spanish American War (1898). The war in Cuba highlighted the desperate and serious need for capable and competent supply services. World War I would have given Howell unprecedented opportunities for travel and would have undoubtedly led him to New York. In New York Howell worked at various odd jobs and likely witnessed the social, cultural and political life of the predominately black section of town Harlem.

Most likely while in New York Howell read *The Holy Piby* and possibly met Robert Athlyi Rogers who authored "*The Blackman's Bible*" as the Piby is often referred in 1924. The Piby is a master theological work that seeks to provide a mythological and biblical foundation for the benefit of the black race.[15] The Piby is considered one of the foundational books of Rastafari. Rogers preached widely in the New York-New Jersey area and founded the Africa Athlican Constructive Church. Howell was a member of *The Universal Negro Improvement Association and African Communities League (UNIA-ACL)* New York and most likely would have met or come in close contact with Marcus Garvey while there. Howell was well known to Garveyites for engaging in nefarious and illegal activities and for his alleged skill as an Obeah or mystic. Undoubtedly Howell learned these religious practices as a direct result of African religious practices that flourished in Jamaica.

Robert Hill noted that it is likely that Howell was deeply influenced by the Communist Party, U.S.A. that operated in New York. During the early to mid 20th century the Communist Party found success in the black community and attracted some of the most prominent members including Trinidadian and rising Party member George Padmore.[16] Howell noted in an interview in November 1940 that prior to establishing the Rastafarian community at "Pinnacle" he led "a socialistic life," which arguably confirms the communist influence.[17] In any case while living in New York Howell would have witnessed the remarkable tenacity of black Americans to establish Harlem as the defacto cultural capital of America. The cultural life of Harlem undoubtedly made an impression on Howell as it did Marcus Garvey.

Howell returned to Jamaica in the 1930s. Why Howell returned to Jamaica is speculative at best. A biographer noted that Howell was arrested for grand larceny and later deported. The source for this came from papers in the Jamaican National Archives in Spanish Town and no mention of his arrest can be found in the New York City Police Records.[18] Nevertheless, Howell could not have timed his return any better. Jamaica had been experiencing a rise of millennialism and by January 1931 the Island Privy Council had drafted a Revivalism Prohibition Law. Millennialism or chiliasm in Greek, is a belief held by many Christian denominations, largely based on *Revelation 20:1–6 that states there will be a Golden Age brought on when the angel will seize the devil or Satan and bound him for a thousand years.*

Notwithstanding internal opposition to the law it signaled the islands growing hostility toward religious movements that existed outside of the government-sanctioned Church. And as I have noted earlier the Church had been perceived as a corrupt institution by many of the lower classes in Jamaica.

At some point Howell began to preach the gospel of H.I.M. Haile Selassie. For example he attempted to sell photos of H.I.M. at Edelweiss Park and was rebuked by Marcus Garvey who kept an ambivalent position toward religious revivalism. Because of Garvey's hostility toward religion Robert Athlyi Rogers had almost denounced Garvey as not a prophet for his strong anti-religious comments.[19] Howell was undoubtedly inspired by the religious revival fervor, especially among the Jamaican poor as his early supporters came from the lower classes of St. Thomas Parish.

By 1933 Howell's religious preaching had been in full swing as he worked to speared the word of the divinity of Ras Tafari Makonnen who had been crowned Haile Selassie Emperor of Ethiopia on November 2, 1930. Howell was one of three men[20] who preached the doctrine that the coronation of Haile Selassie was the fulfillment of a biblical prophecy of Revelations 5:2-5:

> And I saw a strong angel proclaiming with a loud voice, Who is worthy to open the book, and to loose the seals thereof?[3] And no man in heaven, nor in earth, neither under the earth, was able to open the book, neither to look thereon.[4] And I wept much, because no man was found worthy to open and to read the book, neither to look thereon.[5] And one of the elders saith unto me, Weep not: behold, the Lion of the tribe of Judah, the Root of David, hath prevailed to open the book, and to loose the seven seals thereof.

Howell, as well as many other blacks was struck by the lavish and well-attended coronation of Haile Selassie and the number of European heads of state that attended his coronation. Howell and many other early followers of Haile Selassie could only be inspired by a passage in Revelations that seemed to place a man of Africa within its biblical prophecy:

> I saw heaven standing open and there before me was a white horse, whose rider is called Faithful and True. With justice he judges and wages war.[12] His eyes are like blazing fire, and on his head are many crowns. He has a name written on him that no one knows but he himself.[13] He is dressed in a robe dipped in blood, and his name is the Word of God.[14] The armies of heaven

were following him, riding on white horses and dressed
in fine linen, white and clean.[15] *Coming out of his mouth*
is a sharp sword with which to strike down the nations.
"He will rule them with an iron scepter."[a] He treads
the winepress of the fury of the wrath of God Almighty.[16]
On his robe and on his thigh he has this name written:

king of kings and lord of lords.[21]

By 1934 Howell had been preaching that a mass repatriation movement would begin with Jamaicans returning to Ethiopia. Howells' declaration that black Jamaicans should pledge their allegiance to Haile Selassie as and the true leader of the people of Jamaica and Africans world wide infuriated the British government, and arrested and jailed Howell. *The Promised Key* was largely used as evidence against Howell and he spent two years in prison for sedition.

One of the most interesting aspects of Howells's life is the ritual identity that was expressed in the name G.G. *Maragh* that Howell used periodically. When addressed by followers Howell insisted on being addressed by the name *Gangunguru Maragh.* Robert Hill noted that it is most likely that G.G. most likely was composed of Hindi words-*gyan* meaning wisdom, *gun* meaning virtue or talent, and *guru* meaning teacher. The surname of Maragh means great king or king of kings.

The links between Jamaican culture and India extend back to the mid-19ᵗʰ century.

36,000 Indians immigrated to Jamaica as indentured servants between 1845 and 1917. The Indian Government encouraged indentured workers and set up recruiting stations in Calcutta and Madras. Poor Indians were attracted to the Island because of the demand for labor that was due to the end of slavery in 1830.

Most Indians who signed contracts did so in the hope of returning to India with the fruits of their labor, rather than intending to live permanently but nearly two thirds stayed on the Island. One of the cross-cultural exchanges that deeply affected Rastafari culture is the importation of the *Cannabis* plant (Cannabis Indica-Cannabis Sativa) and the religious traditions expressed in the God Shiva and the belief that the plant contains supernatural powers. In any case G.G. Maragh articulated a vision for the early followers of Ras Tafari that has endured for nearly 80 years. Therefore Howell's legacy as one of the first Rastafarians is secure.

Leonard Howell died February 1981 in Kingston, Jamaica.

The Promised Key

In 1935 Howell was serving a two-year term of imprisonment, when he apparently wrote *The Promised Key* under his Hindu pen name G.G. Maragh. A close reading of Howell's work will reveal a close and almost verbatim similarity with an earlier writing by Fitz Balintine Pettersburg, *The*

Royal Parchment Scroll of Black Supremacy (1926). In fact Howell so extensively borrowed from the Royal Parchment that the *Daily Gleaner* warned there was an active movement to spread the idea of Black Supremacy throughout Jamaica.[22]

The text is a straightforward affirmation of what Howell calls black supremacy and the coronation of Ras Tafari as H.I.M. Haile Selassie I. The coronation takes center stage as Howell elaborates on the regal decorum and display of wealth. And the idea that foreign heads of State including a member of the English Royal family offered homage to a black king is a central trope in this work. Howell wrote, *"We can see all the Kings of the earth surrendering their crowns to His Majesty Ras Tafari the King of Kings and Lord of Lords Earth's Rightful Ruler to reign forever and ever."* The coronation was so elaborate that newspaper coverage was disseminated worldwide.

Howell works to instill the idea of the royal linkages of Haile Selassie to that of Solomon and by inference to King David. This is particularly important because many in the west took great measure to point out Haile Selassie's skin color. For example, Time Magazine wrote, *"The complexion and features of Haile Selassie, or Power of Trinity, resemble those of a Spanish Jew. But throughout the world last week Negro news organs hailed him as their own, recalled the honors conferred by His Majesty on "The Black Eagle of Harlem,"*

Colonel Hubert Julian, "The Negro Lindbergh" (see cut). *Matter of fact the people of Ethiopia, or Abyssinia, are of every color from coal black through tawny brown to olive, include many non-Afric races."*[23] For blacks the issue of skin color was mute. It was the idea that Ethiopia, which had long been thought of as the ancient land of black people, was the key factor.

Throughout the text Howell calls forth and praises black supremacy. He noted, *"Black Supremacy has taken charge of white supremacy by King Alpha and Queen Omega the King of Kings. Instead of saying Civilization hereafter we all shall say Black Supremacy. Just takes this drench of indomitable fury and move for the Church triumphant right from the bridge of supreme authority."* This maxim of the inversion of white over black had long been an ideology since slavery was a legal institution in America and the West Indies. For example, legend has it that after the U.S. Civil War in 1865, a black soldier recognized his former master among a group of Confederate prisoners he was guarding and spoke: *"Hello, massa,"* he said, *"bottom rail on top dis time."* Here Howell makes use of the day when black supremacy will prevail over white supremacy.

For religious leaders like Howell and for the number of black intellectuals that watched the Coronation events closely that time had come for blacks to make an accounting of their place on earth and to rise under the banner of *"H.M*

Ras Tafari, King of Kings and Lord of Lords, The Conquering Lion of Judah, The Elect of God and the Light of the world."

Leonard Howell

Marcus Garvey

Haile Selassie & Queen Menen Asfar

The Promised Key
By G. G. Maragh

The Mystery Country

I wish to state to you my dear Readers, that Ethiopia is a Country of great contrasts largely unexplored and is populated by Black People whose attitude towards this so called Western civilization has not changed within the last six thousand years.

The people are Christians while retaining Primitive customs. The result is that the Black People of Ethiopia are extraordinarily blended into a refined fashion that cannot be met with in any other part of the world.

In 1930 the Duke of Gloucester undertook one of the most interesting duties he had been called upon to execute up to this date. The occasion was the Coronation of His Majesty Ras Tafari the King of Kings and Lord of Lords the conquering Lion of Judah, the Elect of God and the Light of the world.

The Duke was to represent his father The Anglo-Saxon King. The Duke handed to His Majesty Rastafari the King of Kings and Lord of lords a Scepter of solid gold twenty seven inches long, which had been taken from the hands of Ethiopia some thousand years ago.

The Duke fell down on bending knees before His Majesty Ras Tafari the King of Kings and Lord of Lords and spoke in a loud voice and said, "Master, Master my father has sent me to represent him sir. He is unable to come and he said that he will serve you to the end Master." See Psalm 72: 9 to 11 verses, also see Gen. 49 chap. 10 verse.

On one side of the Scepter was inscribed Ethiopia shall make her hands reach unto God, and on the other side the King of Kings of Ethiopia, the top of the shaft was finished with a seal and above was a clen cross in which a single carbuncle was set.

The Scepter was a magnificent piece of workmanship and had been designed from an historic piece in which the special ceremonies of His Royal Highness of Ethiopia, Earth's Rightful Ruler.

The Duke also handed to Queen Omega the Empress of Ethiopia a Scepter of gold and ivory. The shaft is in the form of a spray of lilies and at the top a spray of lilies in bloom.

It was a brilliant ceremony, the church began to be filled. The Ethiopians were brilliant in special robes having discarded their precious white robes, and wore Jewels of great value.

The men's swords were being heavily ornamented with gems. On their heads they wore gold braided hats, in which the covered lion's manes were to be seen. In contraction then were the solar note struck by the women who were heavily veiled, and wore heavy cloaks.

His and Her Majesty King Alpha and Queen Omega the King of Kings drove to the Cathedral in a Coach drawn by six white Arab horses.

Queen Omega in a Robe of Silver and the escort on mules wearing lion's skin over their shoulders, forming into procession outside the Cathedral.

King Ras Tafari and Queen Omega the Royal pair, the escort and a line of Bishops and Priests entered the guest rank obeisance.

King Alpha sitting on his Throne homage was done to him by the Bishops and Priests fulfilling the 21st. Psalm. The ceremony took 10 days from the second day to the eleventh day of November 1930.

King Alpha was presented with the orb spurs, and spears and many other mighty emblems of His High Office,

Dignitaries of the world power presented King Alpha with the wealth of oceans.

The Emperor attended to most of his preparations for the reception of his thousands of guests himself, and day after day could be seen rushing about in his scarlet car seeing how the white laborers were getting on with the new road he had ordered that the lawns he had laid down be attended to and that the extension of the electric lights throughout the city were being hurried on.

The False Religion

All the Churches Religious system of today, claims to represent the Lord God of Israel; but the Pope who is satan the devil, false organization is a hypocritical religious system that has three elements, first commercial political and ecclesiastical, to keep the people in ignorance of their wicked course.

Money powers are the great bulwarks of their organization and they use the Religious elements as a smoke screen to keep the people in ignorance of the truth.

The false teachers under the supervision of the Pope of Rome who is satan the devil. The agents of his speaking lies in the churches and let the people walk in darkness.

My dear Readers you can see that all their foundations of the earth are out of course. Allow me to say that there is no throne for the Anglo Saxon white people, they must come down and sit in the dust on the ground there is no throne for them. See Isaiah 47th chapter.

I was angry in my people, I polluted my inheritance and gave them into your hand. I showed no mercy

there will be no one to save you

King Alpha was wroth with us the Black People and had polluted our inheritance for 2520 years and had given us into the hands of the Anglo-Saxon white people, they showed us no mercy therefore evil shall come upon them suddenly.

Now let the Astrologers and Stargazers stand up and save the Anglo-Saxon Kingdom from the vengeance that shall come upon them suddenly.

The Promised Key

The glory that was Solomon greater still reigns in Ethiopia. We can see all the Kings of the earth surrendering their crowns to His Majesty Ras Tafari the King of Kings and Lord of Lords Earth's Rightful Ruler to reign forever and ever.

Upon His Majesty Ras Tafari 's head are many diadems and on His garments a name written King of Kings and Lord of Lords oh come let us adore him for he is King of Kings and Lord of Lords, The Conquering Lion of Judah, The Elect of God and the Light of the world.

His Majesty Ras Tafari is the head over all man for he is the Supreme God. His body is the fullness of him that fillet all in all. Now my dear people let this be our goal, forward to the King of Kings must be the cry of our social hope. Forward to the King of Kings to purify our social standards and our way of living, and rebuild and inspire our character. Forward to the King of Kings to learn the worth of manhood and womanhood. Forward to the King of Kings to learn His code of Laws from the mount demanding absolute Love, Purity, Honesty, and Truthfulness. Forward to the King of Kings to learn His Laws and social order, so that virtue will eventually gain the victory over body and soul and that truth will drive away falsehood and fraud. Members of the King of Kings arise for God's sake and put your armor on.

Dear inhabitants of the Western Hemisphere, the King of Kings warriors can never be defeated, the Pope of Rome and his agents shall not prevail against the King of Kings host warriors you all must stand up, stand up, for the King of Kings.

All ye warriors of the King of Kings lift high King Alpha's Royal Banner, from victory to victory King Alpha shall lead his army till every enemy is vanquished.

Ethiopia's Kingdom

Dear inhabitants of this world King Ras Tafari and Queen Omega are the foundation stones of the Resurrection of the Kingdom of Ethiopia.

Their prayer and labour for our Resurrection is past finding out; no library in this world is able to contain the work of their hands for us, for they work both day and night for our deliverance.

As for this generation of the 20th century you and I have no knowledge how worlds are build and upon what triggers Kingdoms are set.

In King Alpha's Encyclopedia he will explain to us all, how worlds are being built and upon what trigger Kingdoms are set on. He will also explain to us the capacities of generations.

Speaking for the Universe and the womanhood of man Queen Omega the Ethiopian woman is the crown woman of this world. She hands us Her Rule-Book from the poles of supreme authority she is the Cannon Mistress of creation.

King Alpha and Queen Omega are the paymasters of the world, Bible owner and money mint. Do not forget they are Black People if you please.

Owing to the universal rend of our ancient and modern we are at this juncture of our history scattered over the Globe into little sectional groups.

All our local bands throughout the globe are bent towards King Alpha's Royal Repository, the Royal Authority is to admit all Bands, Mission Camps, Denominations into the supreme Royal Repository.

Queen Omega being the balming mistress of many worlds she charges the powerhouse right now.

Ethiopia is the succeeding Kingdom of the Anglo-Saxon Kingdom. A man of greater learning and a better Christian soul, than King Alpha is not to be found on the face of the Globe. He makes the nations heart rejoices with raging joy, we give him the glory. Ethiopia rulebook leads us into different departments of the Kingdom, the records of the Kingdom are with us unto this day. The Regulations points us to the basis of the Kingdom.

Many will not see the truth, because they are spiritually blind. See Matthew 3:13. The woman of Samaria first refused to obey the request of our Lord because she was spiritually blind. But when the great Physician opened up her eyes and healed her of her infirmities concerning her many husbands in the city of Samaria, she found out that her first teachers of denominations throughout the state or country of Samaria were false. Then she cried aloud unto the inhabitants of the city and said Come see a man that told me all that I ever did and is not a native of Samaria but an Hebrew, is not this man the very Christ. Our cities of today are inhabited with the same qualities of people as it was in the days of Jesus and the woman of Samaria.

The Healing

The healing plough of the repository transplanted and rebuilds our very soul and body without fail. The misery of the land is healed by fasting. King Alpha picks us up from out of the midst of the raging misery of the land and hides us from the raging wolves of the land into our Balm Yard. What is a Balm Yard? A Balm Yard is a Holy place that is wholly consecrated to God Almighty for the cleansing and healing of the nations. Where only the Holy Spirit of God alone is allowed to do the Royal work of healing. Who does the balming work? Consecrated men and women that the Holy Spirit moves upon the blazing altar of their soul and endowed them with power that they command and handle the infirmities of the nations.

Have we any authority from King Alpha? Yes we are vessels of the divine honor. Have we any authority from the world? Assuredly yes indeed, King Alpha signs for our destiny and gave us His Supreme Affidavit a trillion centuries after the end of eternal life.

Balm Yard

First and last every soul for admission must be believers in the power of King Ras Tafari the living God.

An admission fee must be paid in advance from four shillings up according to the power and duration of the miserable infirmities whereof one is afflicted (Special Notice).

Sometimes King Alpha has to perform special medical attention.

Royal Notice

King Alpha said Bands are not (run) by Ministers, they are by the Priesthood not after the order of Aaron but strictly after the Royal Order of King Ras Tafari the King of Kings of Ethiopia.

Revivalists are not common people, if some individuals of the lower order in the dung heap happen to get into the world by mistake he or she will soon get out and hang him or herself. The reason why revivalists would have not been lightened up with radiance before now, King Alpha was awaiting for the Delegates of the Resurrection of the Kingdom of Ethiopia and King Alpha's work is strictly perfect and He and Queen Omega do not business with Anglo-Militant white people nakedness.

King Alpha said that a Balm Yard is not a Hospital neither is it a obeah shop. People that are guilty of obeah must not visit balm yards nor in the Assembly of Black Supremacy. No admittance for Fortunetellers witch and old hag. No admittance for obeah dogs none whatever, no admittance for ghost, witch, lizards, no admittance for Alligators, Snakes, Puss, Crabs, Flies, Ants, Rats, and Mice, and Lodestones, Pin, and Needles, John Crows, the Ravens and Candles, fast Cups and Rum Bottles and Grave Yards are not required.

People's clothes, a beast hair and fowls and Grave dirt not wanted. The Woman's baby will strive in her belly, and your Snake and Lizards will not be able to hurt her. For your ghosts will come right back to you. For this is Ethiopia's balm yard and we do not have leprosy. For ghosts only visit the leper's home.

This poison is for all bad spirits it is No. 666 it is good for the Pope of Rome and the Monarch of hell bottom you will not be here to grudge, or obeah, or rob the people nor breed up the young girls and treat them like dog.

You will not plant your obeah self with no man or woman so that we who are King Alpha's children cannot get rid of you until the obeah rotten. Science my dear King your black and white heart obeah factory is up side down. Take this ramkin dose of fatal deadly poison and leave for God's sake do it quickly. By Supreme law of King Alpha the King of Kings, you will not blind, give big foot or sore, or turn any more children across the woman's belly and kill her baby when it is born, nor any time after. Every good looking man's wife you see you want to cohabit with her, you rotten gut snake, and anywhere a man put a business you go there to kill and drive away, you dead cold horse.

This pole is Black Supremacy owned by King Alpha the King of Kings now Ethiopia knew the perfect value of Holy Baptism under water, for King Alpha taught us how to appreciate the power of holy baptism.

Now we the Black People have no pardon to beg white supremacy, no favor to ask her for she is an acknowledged deceiver. From B.C. 4001 to A. D. second score, she faked all Christianity.

Black Supremacy the Church Triumphant has denounced her openly for baptism is a very important subject to Black Supremacy.

How to Fast

The King of Kings of creation the first and last said "Blessed are they that searcheth the deep things on the tree of life for His wisdom is deep and is past all finding out."

Thus said the living God and owner of life, to overcome white bondage and filth and black hypocrisy amongst your own black skin you have to fast hard or the white man is very filthy and the black man is an hypocrite and hypocrite means a crook, a filthy man that class of white folks who cut with the crook they are called Black-White.

Always have a basin of fine or coarse salt on your fast table as long as God is your ruler. When you break your fast do not throw the water over your heads the trouble will fall on you. When you are all ready with your cup in hand the Elder will ask is it all well with thee, everybody shall say together all is well with me Then the Elder shall ask again "Who will bear a true witness for the Tree of Life?" All shall say by the Living God will God help me for life, and the leader shall say follow me with your cup of trouble to the burying place of sin and shame.

Then everybody walk quietly and respectfully throw away the water, then come in and wash your hands and face and be happy feeling satisfied and revived and lovely. House to house fasting is very powerful, it lifts the work and removes devils from homes of those in distress. Once a week for the general assembly is all right. A love feast every three or six months is needed.

Department

Mount Africa the world's capital, the new Bible land, the triumphant lot is for King Alpha own lot until this day. Slave Traders called the world's capital, Jamaica British West Indies. Before the Adamic deadly diseases poisoned the human family with fallen Angels, blue murders, there has been only one perfect language on the face of the globe. Therefore the Anglo Militant fallen Angel tongues are not appreciated by His Majesty King Alpha the Monarch of Life. Thus said Ras Tafari the living God to creation vast Rome has deceived the race of man, and has killed the mortal supreme monarch Ethiopia's glory is no guesser long before this world was Ethiopia's glory has been running Con-trillion of centuries ago.

Ethiopia's Repository will change and qualify the fallen Angels deadly poisonous indomitable lying tongue. Stupidity is the most they get out of the various tongues spoken by the majority. Ninety-five out of every one hundred do not know what they do or say any ghost can fool them at any corner.

Government

Black Supremacy has taken charge of white supremacy by King Alpha and Queen Omega the King of Kings. Instead of saying Civilization hereafter we all shall say Black Supremacy. Just takes this drench of indomitable fury and move for the Church triumphant right from the bridge of supreme authority.

Black Supremacy will promote the mortals of every shade according to our powers to go. The Black Museum will be opened day and night for life. Education will be free and compulsory to all mortal beings, if you are not an enemy of black Supremacy,

Man and women can marry right in School if you are of a respectable proportion of dignity. Black must not marry white nor white black, race enmity. (see p. 40)

Always be a respectful diplomat, always give an intelligent reply to every person that approach or write you on any subject always ask for the full value inside the nature of any written subject. Do not put your quick judgment on any person confidence is quick to move, just what the people are that is just the state of your government. Do not follow the Court House and Doctors they will fake you to death. Do not marry any divorced person it is a curse, stick to your own wife and husband.

Do not watch and peep your wife or husband, you are only digging a grave for yourself. Do not try to make your wife or husband or family feel small because you have got more college filth in your head, hold them up, they are the cause of you being what you are. I know thousands of college hogs and dogs, professional swine's; also some very fine people.

Eternal Law Office

His and Her Majesty King Alpha and Queen Omega said that they do not call ministers to Black Supremacy banquets for ministers are not working for him they are following Adam Abraham Anglo-Saxon the leper. Legislators said one man cannot serve two masters.

Adam Abraham the leper is boss for ministers and lawyers because all they teach and preach about is Adam-Eve and Abraham the leper. For they do not see one book in the Bible written by Adam and Eve or the book of Abraham or book of Isaac. According to the clearness of this case there is nobody name Adam Eve and Abraham.

If you ever touch the slave papers they catch you sure as His Majesty Ras Tafari lives. The officers and soldiers at camp that have power and influence are well posted by King Alpha the King of Kings, their names you will not know. Legislators said one man cannot serve two masters. Ministers say they can't work with Adam and Eve and work for King Alpha and Queen Omega the same time. Abraham the historian said despise the both of them; lawyers said you got to find fault with them, the judges said leave the Alpha and Omega out, because they are black and skin for skin.

Eve the Mother of Evil

The Adamic tree of knowledge and Eve the mother of Evil, see Genesis 2nd chapter. The Adamic apple tree my dear leper your name is Adam-Abraham Anglo-Saxon apple tree, that look pretty and respectable to your eyes don't it? Yes indeed--gross beauty is the Queen in hell, and Royal leper Adam and Eve and Abraham and Anglo-Saxon are all white people if you please.

King Alpha and Queen Omega said they are Black Arch Sovereign of most Holy Times, and perfect Virginity, and Supreme Crown Head of Holy Times The Pay Master and keeper of the Perfect Tree of Life and creators of Creation, Dynasties and Kingdoms, Holy Genealogy and Holy Theocracy and Celestial in Terrestrial Mediator if you wish to know their profession.

The Eternal Come Back King Alpha the Monarch Sovereign Pay-Master and Owner of this world. Just make one Eternal come back at His Pay Office.

King Alpha and his wife Queen Omega were here on earth before if you please. Old Alpha the Lion of Creation said to Queen Omega please hand me the Pay Roll and the Militant and Balance Sheet. And your Majesty will mount His Excellency's Great Circle Throne and throw Old Theocracy above the Wheel of Holy Time, right into Holy Eternity to the Lion of Alpha and Omega the King of kings forevermore.

King Alpha and Queen Omega are Black People if you please. They are commonly called the Exodus if you please, the book of Exodus is theirs if you please. Notice if you see Moses and Aaron and Abraham gave any strong report of King Alpha and Queen Omega in their fake Bible if you please. Well since a man has right to pay without work, this world can also work with pay.

There is no book in the Bible for the Anglo Saxon Creation, there is no book of Isaac or his father Abraham in the New Testament.

King Alpha the Most Sacred and Everlasting God, Heaven and Earth's creator, said that Adam Abraham-Anglo Saxon whit people are not entitled to any eternal reward according to his schedule.

My dear Ethiopians, Ethiopia is the crown head of this earth field since heaven has been built by His Majesty Ras Tafari the living God. Thank and praise the ever-living God as long as eternal ages roll.

King Alpha and Queen Omega said they are our parents, and the keeper of the Tree of Life. He and his wife are not any family at all to Adam and Eve and Abraham and Isaac and the Anglo Saxon Slave Owners; for that is exactly how His Majesty King Noah the Black Monarch was drowned at Antediluvia by Adam Abraham the Anarchy.

Judge Samson lost his tribunal and life by marrying the Philistine white woman. See Judges 14, 15 and 10th chapters. See how the Philistine Judges plotting out riddles with the woman how to get him.

The Rapers

The AMERICAN rapers Klu-Klux-Klan and Mob Lynching policy! These unfortunate ones are the outcome of the advance Rate on the Anglo-Saxon slave train. The Advance Rate means—in time of slavery, the white slave masters committed boisterous fornication with the black woman that were taken slaves.

In those days the black men held no opportunity to (Rate) that is, to lie with white women. Therefore, while the black men's blood was burning up in their bodies for the sexual support of their own women the white slave masters took away all the best black women and committed boisterous fornication with them and called it Advance Rate. That is how the third class people came into the human vein.

In those days this act was called the Advance Rate of white supremacy; it is the universal spirit of abuse that manifests itself that the common class black man are now raping the common class white woman.

Both rapers and mob lynchers and Klu-Klux Klan are to be shot down from off the face of God Almighty's beautiful earth.

Ethiopian Question

The Ethiopian Question is this: The continent of Ethiopia is that national. She is that rich national woman that has charmed the men of nations to be with her.

After a time when they all have lived and cohabited with her they all broke her down and left her and persecuted her.

That is just how all nations manage to soak through the Ethiopian woman of prosperity. She had too much sympathy for the perishing nations whose lives are riotously lived until this day.

Slave traders went into Ethiopia and damaged her seeds, beyond any earthly cure. Because she had too much sympathy for willful idlers of various nations. They went into her robbed her lands, money and took her seeds to be slaves.

Today she and her children have no power in her own land, or abroad. All that Ethiopians have to do now, is build anew. Get out a new dictionary and a new Bible, and a new

Board of Education and Money Mint. The outfit shall be called Black supremacy; signed by His and Her Majesty Ras Tafari and Queen omega the King of Kings, head of this world.

The lesson learnt by slave traders through Black Histories is well preserved. We have given our blood, souls, bodies and spirits to redeem Adam Abraham Anglo Saxon the white A. D. second score at his astonishing stop. He is still infested with indomitable, incurable, accursed, deadly disease. We have given him access to the tree of life, we gave him the Garden of Eden, we gave him Egypt, we gave them Daniel and the body of the Black Virgin, the mother of Jesus and they took Joseph also.

We gave ourselves to be slaves for hundred of years. We gave up King Alpha and Queen Omega the first and the last. Now we are disgusted with them, we wash our hands of them for life.

The First and the Last

His Majesty Ras Tafari alone with his bona-fide Lion hearted wife Queen Omega King of Kings, most Living and Eternal, and Ever Living Sovereign owner of Life, the Biblical Sovereign of this World.

His Majesty Ras Tafari the Bible Owner of Holy Times denounced the Bible Militant also the Militant Dictionary. And take off the Black man, his posterity's from off the

Anglo Militant Slave Train at Nationality and planted the Church Triumphant.

The Black Supremacy on triumphant soil the world's capital the new Bible Land, the isles of Springs the same country that the Anarchy called Jamaica British West Indies. Black Supremacy's greatest men and women are sub-ways and air masters of every shade, they sleep in bed and eat with you, and you do not know what triggers your life and destiny is on the Gods of laws are my students said the King of Kings, the air you are breathing this minute is for King Ras Tafari. The barbed wire eternity is his; the brimstone is his. I want you to know that the firmament is his. When He speaks to her she obeys His Royal Voice, His and Her Majesty Ras Tafari and Queen Omega and we the Black People that is King Alpha and Queen Omega seeds will be here in gross prosperity as soon as the Anglo Saxon white peoples all die out if you please.

King Alpha and Queen Omega are the typesetters for time and eternity if you please. The keeper of the tree of life, owner of the Zodiac, owner of this earth; they are the Ethiopian Kingdom owner, if you please. Adam Abraham Anglo-Saxon the leper has no place in this earth if you please

Matrimonial Affidavit

His Majesty Ras Tafari said: now sweetheart my dear wonder, just take this drench of perfect wonders and live with me for life. His Majesty King Alpha and Queen Omega being the keepers of the tree of life Dear heart before we take charge of the Guest Chamber of Creation He said that they had to clear God's perfect reputation and the tree of life. They are requested to call the medical powerhouse of this world and have their best physicians to (loose) the Virgin matrix and give them a crown diploma of our dignity.

The Royal name of this Ethiopian dignity is called Black Supremacy, by the Sacred Order of His Majesty Ras Tafari the living Creator, the living God, and Earth Superior, the master builder of Creation, the perfect Royal Head of this World.

King Ras Tafari and Queen Omega the King of Kings and Lord of Lords, the conquering Lion of Judah, the Elect of God and the Light of the World, the First and the Last, the beginning and ending.

Black People Black People Arise and Shine

Black People, Black People arise and shine for the light has come and the glory of the King of Kings is now risen upon thee. Let not the preachers of the white man's doctrine persuade you to turn your back against H. M. Ras Tafari the Lord God of Israel. Every man was created for the earth in order that he might have and enjoy the fullness of the richness of the Earth.

44

The white man's doctrine has forced the black man to forsake silver and gold and seek Heaven after death. It has brought us to live in disgrace and die in dishonor. Now we the black man have found out that their doctrine was only a trick, and all their intention was to make themselves strong and to fool the black man.

As I G. G. Maragh speak unto you, this is a very serious affair and must not be forsaken. The wise black man woman and children gaining knowledge diligently toward the truth of H. M. Ras Tafari Kingdom must be had before one could possibly receive the truth, for he is King of Kings and Lords of Lords, therefore he is earth's rightful ruler. In this name alone will the black people receive happiness. His throne is forever and ever and a Scepter of righteousness is the Scepter of his Kingdom.

Woe be unto the preacher of the white man's doctrine a hypocrisy or devil worship. There are millions of persons of good will who see the cruel unjust and wicked things done in the Church organizations in the name of God.

It is the will of H. M. Ras Tafari that such persons of good will may have an opportunity to get knowledge of truth. May I state that all reasonable persons who hear the truth should readily see that the Pope of Rome and his preachers are Ras Tafari who is the Lord God of Israel's great opposer and greatest enemy. Persons of good will to the Kingdom of H. I. M. will live forever. The other[s] will remain dead forever.

Woe be unto them that forsaketh H. M. Ras Tafari as being God Almighty, they shall be cast into hell both body and soul.

PEACE BE UNTO YOU, PEACE BE UNTO YOU.

Forward to the King of Kings by L. Howell

His Majesty Ras Tafari is the head over all man for he is the Supreme God. His body is the fullness of him that fillet all in all.

Now my dear people let this be our goal:

Forward to the King of Kings must be the cry of our social hope.

Forward to the King of Kings to purify our social standards and our way of living, and rebuild and inspire our character.

Forward to the King of Kings to learn the worth of manhood and womanhood.

Forward to the King of Kings to learn His code of Laws from the mount demanding absolute Love, Purity, Honesty, and Truthfulness.

Forward to the King of Kings to learn His Laws and social order, so that virtue will eventually gain the victory over body and soul and that truth will drive away falsehood and fraud.

Members of the King of Kings arise for God's sake and put your armor on.

Endnotes

1. Leonard E. Barrett, *The Rastafarians: A Study in Messianic Cultism in Jamaica*, (Puerto Rico: Institute of Caribbean Studies, 1969), 69.

2. St. Clair Drake, *The Redemption of Africa and Black Religion*, (Chicago: Third World Press, 1970), 18.

3. Laurent Dubois, *Avengers of the New World: The Story of the Haitian Revolution*, (Cambridge: The Belknap Press, 2004), 18.

4. Richard B. Sheridan, *"Sweet Malefactor": The Social Costs of Slavery and Sugar in Jamaica and Cuba, 1807-54*, The Economic History Review, vol. 29, no. 2, (May 1976), 239.

5. Ibid, 14.

6. Orlando Patterson, *The Sociology of Slavery: An Analysis of the Origins, Developments and Structure of Negro Slave Society in Jamaica*, (Rutherford: Fairleigh Dickinson University Press, 1975), 15.

7. Ibid, 9.

8. Ibid, 39.

9. Ibid, 40.

10. Ibid, 70.

11. Ibid, 208.

12. Ibid, 210.

13. Barrett, 26.

14. See Robert Hill, *Dread History: Leonard P. Howell and Millenarian Visions on the Early Rastafarian Religion*, (Chicago: Research Associates School Times, 2001), 22 and Helene Lee, *The First Rasta: Leonard Howell and the Rise of Rastafarianism*, (Chicago: Chicago Review Press), 17.

15. See W. Gabriel Selassie I, "Introduction & Analysis," In *The Holy Piby*, Rob Athlyi Rogers, (Los Angeles: Orunmilla, Inc., 2015).

16. George Padmore (1903 –1959), born Malcolm Ivan Meredith Nurse in Trinidad, was a leading Pan-Africanist, journalist, and author who left Trinidad in 1924 to study in the United States and from there moved to the Soviet Union, Germany, and France, before settling in London and, toward the end of his life, Accra, Ghana.

17. Hill, 23. In November 1940 a newspaper reporter met Howell and interviewed Howell at Pinnacle. The newspaper reporter stated that the Pinnacle settlement contained over 700 men and women "forming a socialist colony." See also Louis Moyston, *Pinnacle: The Truth About the Matter,* Jamaican Observer, Feb. 04, 2014.

18. Lee, 297.

19. Selassie I, "Introduction & Analysis."

20. Howell along with Joseph Hibbert, Archibald Dunkley, and Robert Hinds began preaching the idea that Haile Selassie was the Messiah returned to earth. See Robert Hill, *The Marcus Garvey Papers and the Universal Negro Improvement Association Papers, Volume VII,* (Los Angeles: University of California, 1990) 602.

21. Revelations (KJV) 19:11-16.

22. Hill, 18.

23. Time Magazine, 30 Nov 1930.

Printed in Great Britain
by Amazon